D1370705

MONTGOMERY:
LAUNCHING THE CIVIL RIGHTS MOVEMENT

Linda R. Wade

ROURKE ENTERPRISES, INC.
Vero Beach, FL 32964

Library of Congress Cataloging-in-Publication Data

Wade, Linda R.
Montgomery: launching the civil rights movement/by Linda R. Wade.
p. cm. — (Doors to America's past)

Includes index.
Summary: Describes the history of Montgomery, Alabama, and the events which roused public opinion throughout the country in support of the civil rights movement.
ISBN 0-86592-465-1
1. Montgomery (Ala.) – Race relations – Juvenile literature.
2. Afro-Americans – Civil rights – Alabama – Montgomery – Juvenile literature. 3. Civil rights movements – Alabama – Montgomery – History – 20th century – Juvenile literature. [1. Montgomery (Ala.) – Race relations.
2. Afro-Americans – Civil rights – Alabama – Montgomery. 3. Civil rights movements – Alabama – Montgomery.] I. Title II. Series: Wade, Linda R. Doors to America's past.
F334.M79W33 1991
305.896'073076147—dc20
90-8974
CIP
AC

Acknowledgments
Special thanks to the staff of the Alabama Archives and History Museum; Dr. Frederick D. Reese, Principal of Selma High School; Bobby Jackson, World Heritage Museum; Mary Alice Neeley, Old Alabama Town; and Anna Bishop, Jamie Wallace, Edie Morthland Jones, David Waymire, and the many people who supplied information and pictures.

Photo Credits
Alabama Department of Archives and History, Montgomery, Alabama: 5, 7, 9, 14, 28 (right), 43 (right)
Landmarks Foundation of Montgomery: 46
Lyndon Baines Johnson Library and Museum: 36
Montgomery Area Chamber of Commerce: cover, 16, 33, 40, 41, 43 (left), 45
Selma and Dallas County Chamber of Commerce: 1, 28 (left), 30, 37

Table of Contents

Introduction

On February 18, 1861, Jefferson Davis climbed the steps of the Capitol Building in Montgomery, Alabama, where he took the oath of office to become President of the Confederate States of America. As head of the southern Confederacy, he would guide it in the Civil War, the bloody struggle between the North and the South. The War Between the States, as it was also called, was fought over the issues of slavery and states' rights.

One hundred and four years later, in 1965, Dr. Martin Luther King, Jr., climbed the same Capitol Building steps. He had just led 25,000 civil rights marchers down Montgomery's Dexter Avenue. The demonstrators were bringing to a close a historic civil rights march from Selma, Alabama, 50 miles away, to Montgomery. The purpose of the march was to protest the many barriers that still existed to keep black people from voting.

From those same steps in Montgomery where Davis had once proclaimed the right of slavery to exist, King now gave a powerful voice to the movement that would bring equal rights to all Americans. For Montgomery, often called the Cradle of the Confederacy, was also

Inauguration of Jefferson Davis at Montgomery, Alabama on February 18, 1861

destined to become a cradle of the modern civil rights movement.

In what ways did history call this Alabama city to help change the definition of freedom for African-Americans, and, finally, for all Americans? In what ways has Montgomery been the birthplace of modern civil rights, in spite of some resistance that is yet to be overcome in America?

Let's travel to Montgomery, capital of the Old South, and a recognized leader of the New South.

1

Early Struggles for Equal Rights

The struggle for civil rights for all Americans began long before the founding of Montgomery, Alabama. In the early 1600s, Africans were brought to America and sold as slaves. The system of slavery continued for 250 years.

Many slave owners treated their slaves cruelly in order to keep them in their lowly place. Many slaves were given no education, and risked death if they tried to escape. But the yearning for freedom and a better life survived in the hearts of these captives.

Though inviting death if caught, occasionally a slave managed to escape and help other black people on the path to freedom.

Harriet Tubman was such a woman. In 1849, she escaped from slavery by way of the underground railroad, a system run by freed slaves and white supporters. Not an actual railroad, it was a network of homes along the way where fleeing slaves hid while secretly being taken North to freedom.

The operation was dangerous and illegal. Tubman made 19 rescue missions to the South, however, helping

A black slave family in front of their cabin

hundreds of slaves to escape. Using her remarkable ingenuity and bravery, she never was caught, nor did she ever lose a slave.

Harriet Tubman went on to serve the North during the Civil War as a nurse and scout. Later she helped build schools for blacks, and gave other assistance to needy black people.

Frederick Douglass was another slave who became a renowned promoter of equal rights for blacks. Fleeing a cruel master, he taught himself to read and write with some help from a kindly white mistress. In 1838, he escaped North. A gifted speaker, writer, editor, and organizer, Douglass devoted his life to fighting for black people's rights.

Sojourner Truth, another former slave, became one of the best-known speakers of her day. She helped free other slaves, and in 1843, began traveling widely throughout the Northeast and Midwest, urging the abolition of slavery. She also worked in Washington, D.C., to improve life for black people there.

Another black man, W.E.B. Dubois, spoke eloquently and wrote extensively about racial discrimination. A distinguished scholar, Dubois was, in 1895, the first black person to receive a Ph.D. degree from Harvard. Believing that blacks needed to demand equal rights, he helped found the National Association for the Advancement of Colored People (NAACP) in 1910.

Early champions of freedom such as these served to inspire their fellow blacks and other Americans. With the election of Abraham Lincoln as president in 1861, the stage was set to abolish slavery. Lincoln's Emancipation Proclamation of 1863 freed some slaves, many of whom then fought and died for the North in the Civil War. Later, passage of constitutional amendments brought greater provisions for freedom. The 13th amendment, passed in

Slaves picking cotton on a southern plantation

1865, outlawed slavery. The 14th amendment (1866) protected the rights of newly freed slaves, and the 15th amendment (1870) gave black citizens the right to vote.

But these promises were not kept. Most white people in the South did not want blacks to be free. After the Civil War, a group of Confederate Army veterans formed the Ku Klux Klan (KKK). It used terrorism and violence to achieve its goal of white supremacy—power for white people only. Other individuals and groups supported the same ends.

Between 1882 and 1901, nearly 2,000 blacks were lynched—carried away and hung by a mob. States passed laws requiring black people to use separate restrooms, water fountains, restaurants, schools, waiting rooms, swimming pools, libraries, and bus seats. The discriminatory laws were called "Jim Crow" laws, after a black minstrel in a song that was popular at the time.

Nor was the federal government yet committed to equal justice for all. In an 1896 case, the Supreme Court ruled that separate facilities for black people were legal so long as they were equal. But in many areas of the South, equal facilities were not provided, only separate ones.

George Henry White, the only black U.S. Congressman at the turn of the century, spoke out against racism. A former slave, he sponsored the first anti-lynching law, and urged the government to enforce the constitutional amendments that guaranteed equal rights to blacks. But the letter of the law continued to be quite different from the actual practice of it. As black people began organizing for reform, many white people strengthened their opposition. During the 1920s, the KKK and other white supremacists became more violent. Many KKK members held high positions in government throughout the country, and KKK membership swelled to two million.

Many blacks moved North, hoping to escape KKK terrorism and to find better jobs. For those blacks who stayed behind, not much hope existed for the promises of freedom as other Americans knew it.

2
Some Improvements

With the election of President Franklin Roosevelt in 1932, the lives of black people improved. Jobs and welfare became available to both blacks and whites as part of the New Deal. The New Deal was the president's reform program to help the U.S. recover from the terrible economic collapse—the Great Depression—that the country was experiencing in the early '30s.

Further labor gains were made for blacks through the efforts of A. Philip Randolph. A well-known black labor leader, he convinced President Roosevelt to ban racial discrimination in all defense industries.

After World War II, the demand for equal rights found another voice. Black soldiers returning from fighting against Nazi racism and oppression were more aware than ever that they themselves were the victims of racism at home. With increased pressure from black soldiers and leaders, President Harry Truman ended segregation in the armed forces in 1945. Black and white soldiers would then live and fight together, not in segregated, or separate, units.

In addition, many civil rights activists in the 1940s were inspired by that era's famous Indian leader, Mohandas Gandhi. Gandhi's philosophy called for peaceful demonstrations against unjust laws. Using Gandhi's nonviolent approach to reform, India's masses were making moves toward freedom from their oppressors. In 1942, encouraged by Gandhi's accomplishments, a group of black Americans formed a nonviolent civil rights group called the Congress of Racial Equality (CORE). Its members entered "white only" restaurants in the North and sat quietly, even when harassed or attacked. As a result, restaurants in a few northern cities became integrated— they served both black and white customers. But the South held firm to old segregation practices.

Civil rights groups such as CORE, the NAACP, and others were able to erase some barriers against black people. But the major victories against segregation would take place in the federal courts. In 1950, NAACP lawyers began building a legal case to abolish segregated schools. Anything less would be contrary to the U.S. Constitution, the lawyers concluded. Until that time, some local school districts had improved black schools because of pressure from black groups. Now, the call would be for the complete integration of black and white schools, not just an improvement in black schools.

3

The Beginning of Change

Black parents all over the country wanted their children to get a good education, but black schools were generally run-down and poorly equipped. Furthermore, many black children had to ride buses great distances every day to get to their black schools, even though better white schools existed in their own neighborhoods.

Seven-year-old Linda Brown of Topeka, Kansas, was such a black child. NAACP lawyers used her case and three others to represent millions of black children in America. The lawyers prepared their legal arguments that segregation was unconstitutional, and then took their case to court. They lost. But they did not give up. The lawyers then took the case to the Supreme Court in Washington, D.C. There they were successful.

On May 17, 1954, the Supreme Court, the highest court in the land, handed down a landmark decision in the case known as *Brown v. Board of Education.* As everyone waited tensely in the Supreme Court chambers for the verdict, the Chief Justice read the decision: "To separate black children solely because of their race generates a feeling of inferiority as to their status in the community

Two black children with their mule

that may affect their hearts and minds in a way very unlikely ever to be undone.... Separate educational facilities are...unequal."

Many white people in the South were enraged at the court's decision. Black people, however, rejoiced. Filled with a new spirit of hope, they quickly took the next steps toward freedom. Four days after the Supreme Court ruling, Jo Ann Robinson, a black resident of Montgomery, wrote a letter to the mayor of that city.

She said she represented a large group of black women who wanted fair treatment on city buses. Black people made up 75 percent of the city's bus riders, yet they were required to sit in the back of buses where seats were designated "colored." Furthermore, when all the "white" seats were full, black people had to give up their seats to white people. The mayor responded by arguing that segregation was the law, and that he could not change it.

On December 1, 1955, Rosa Parks, a Montgomery black woman, made an important decision. She was returning from work that day when the driver stopped the bus and ordered Mrs. Parks and three other black people to give up their seats to white people. The three other blacks got up, but a tired Mrs. Parks kept her seat. She was arrested.

It was not the first time that a black person had been arrested on a Montgomery bus. But Mrs. Parks was well-known and liked in the black community, where people were outraged at the unfair treatment of the woman.

When Jo Ann Robinson learned of the incident, she and her group immediately concluded that the time had come for a bus boycott. In the boycott, all black people would refuse to ride buses until they would be treated

Dexter Avenue Baptist Church, later re-named Dexter Avenue King Memorial Baptist Church to honor Dr. King.

fairly. Without passengers, the bus company would lose money and might be forced to negotiate with the protestors.

Other blacks in the city quickly formed a group called the Montgomery Improvement Association. For their leader they selected a young man who had recently accepted his first pastorate in a local black church. His name was Dr. Martin Luther King, Jr.

Four days later, on the evening of December 5, Dr. King spoke to a large crowd of people who had gathered to hear the young preacher. "There comes a time that people get tired," he told them, "...tired of being segregated and humiliated....We have no alternative but to protest." In his speech, he also called for the practice of nonviolence, a philosophy he would urge all of his life.

The protest—the bus boycott—lasted 381 days. During that time, the 17,500 black people of Montgomery who usually rode the bus every day did not do so. Instead, they walked, took black taxis, used car pools, borrowed cars—some even rode mules—and always they remained nonviolent, even when harassed and beaten by angry whites.

On December 21, 1956, just about a year later, Montgomery's blacks at last won their battle: the Supreme Court outlawed bus segregation. Montgomery's black people had shown the world what a nonviolent protest could accomplish. They had shown the world that the civil rights struggle was a movement of all black people—whole cities of black people.

Many historians believe that the Montgomery bus boycott, as the first mass action of black people, was the beginning of the modern civil rights movement in the U.S.

4
Schools, Lunch Counters, Buses, and Jail

If the Montgomery bus boycott was difficult, the days of integrating schools would be much worse. To comply with the Supreme Court ruling, many southern cities undertook school integration by using their own police and local leadership. In other southern locations, however, federal troops were needed to protect black children. When nine black students entered high school in Little Rock, Arkansas in September 1957, white opposition was so great that President Eisenhower had to use U.S. troops to walk the children to and from school all year long.

The intervention of federal troops in Little Rock did not end the struggle for integration. It did, however, show that the federal government would not allow defiance of federal law. In 1962, when James Meredith became the first black student to attend the University of Mississippi, President John Kennedy ordered federal troops to protect him.

Alabama Governor George Wallace met with the same response from the federal government. In January 1963, he tried to prevent the admission of a black student to the University of Alabama, and later he tried to prevent the integration of public elementary and secondary schools. In both cases, President Kennedy sent in the National Guard to enforce the integration law.

Most civil rights activists at the time realized that, to keep their demands in the public eye, blacks needed to keep confronting white people in a nonviolent way. Evidence supporting that view was an incident that had occurred and made news headlines in Greensboro, North Carolina in 1960. Four black college students had walked into a Woolworth's store, sat down at the lunch counter, and ordered coffee. The waitress told them, "We don't serve colored here." The four young men peacefully sat there until the store closed.

The next day, the four were joined by 19 other black students. By the end of the week, 400 students, including several whites, were sitting quietly in shifts at the lunch counter. The following week, seven other North Carolina cities became the scene of similar sit-ins. The sit-ins, as they were called, captured the attention of young people all over the South. They soon staged sit-ins in more than 100 southern cities—in restaurants, parks, swimming pools, libraries, and theaters. Within a year, about 70,000 people had participated in sit-ins, and 3,600 had been arrested. Many, especially in the Deep South, were beaten and terrorized. But the response of the protestors continued to be nonviolent.

Other black activists set out to test a Supreme Court order that outlawed segregation in bus terminals. Called the Freedom Riders, they continually met with brutal resistance. So violent were the attacks on them that once again the federal government had to intervene, ordering the bus companies to integrate their terminals.

Demonstrations continued in the '60s. Birmingham, Alabama, one of the South's most segregated cities at the time, became the scene of bitter struggles. Even Martin Luther King, Jr. was jailed there when he tried to lead a boycott in the city. While in jail, he wrote a now-famous letter to those who suggested that he be more patient in the pursuit of civil rights. "I guess it is easy," he wrote, "for those who have never felt the stinging darts of segregation to say, 'Wait.' But freedom is never voluntarily given by the oppressor; it must be demanded by the oppressed."

Even school children joined the Birmingham demonstrations. On May 3, 1963, thousands of young people— some no more than six years of age—faced police dogs and fire hoses. Some were arrested. News cameras filmed the scenes and broadcast them on national TV. Americans were shocked, and President Kennedy quickly sent federal mediators to work out agreements.

The struggle in Birmingham was especially bloody. Repeatedly terrorized, many blacks started to abandon the philosophy of peaceful resistance, and fought back. Dr. King, in some of his most trying hours, personally walked the streets of the city for days, pleading with blacks to forsake the violence. But the struggle in Birmingham ended in victory. Through federal mediation, the city's businessmen agreed to integrate downtown stores and other facilities and to hire more black people. The victory also gave new courage to the civil rights movement. It showed the federal government's growing determination to enforce its anti-discrimination laws.

5

A Civil Rights Bill

In June 1963, a month after Birmingham, President Kennedy sent a civil rights bill to Congress. Excitement grew in the civil rights movement. In August, 250,000 blacks and whites marched on Washington, D.C., in support of the proposed bill. During the demonstration, Dr. King gave a speech—his now-famous "I Have a Dream" speech—from the front of the Lincoln Memorial. He spoke of his dream for "all of God's children...to join hands and sing...'Free at last, free at last; thank God Almighty, we are free at last!' "

The speech was one of the high points of the civil rights movement. Then, public support for the civil rights act grew even more rapidly in the next two months when two events occurred: a dynamite explosion in a Birmingham church killed four black Sunday school students; and in November, President Kennedy was assassinated. The time had come to bring about change in America.

The following summer, Congress passed the Civil Rights Act of 1964, the strongest civil rights bill in U.S. history. It ordered restaurants and other places of business that serve the general public to serve all people regardless of race, color, religion, or national origin. It outlawed discrimination in employment, and created an agency to enforce fair practices in the workplace. The act also stated that the government would cut off federal funds from any activity that continued policies of racial discrimination.

But in spite of the gains of the Civil Rights Act, there still were many complicated and unfair restrictions that kept black people from voting. Yet, only by having voting power would black people be able to keep pressure on the government to protect their newly gained rights.

Registering to vote and voting had always been difficult, even dangerous, for black people in most of the South. Easing the way to the voting booth would be the next big challenge for black Americans. That challenge was taken up immediately. The summer of the passage of the Civil Rights Act became known as "Freedom Summer." Thousands of college students, most of them white, went to Mississippi to register black voters. Many people believed that if white volunteers were attacked for voting activities, the country would take notice.

They were right. On the first day of Freedom Summer, three young men—two white and one black—were killed. Michael Schwerner and Andrew Goodman, civil rights workers from the North, and James Chaney, a southern black activist, were kidnapped and murdered. By the end of the summer, 80 civil rights workers had been beaten and more that 1,000 arrested, 37 black churches had been burned, and 30 homes bombed.

America could no longer ignore the cruelty of racial hatred. What would happen next?

6

The Teachers March

In January 1965, the new president, Lyndon Johnson, made a speech to Congress. Strongly voicing the government's support of civil rights, he promised black Americans enforcement of the Civil Rights Law and the elimination of barriers to the right to vote.

Black leaders quickly took the opportunity to support the president's promise. They would show just how difficult it was to register black voters.

Dr. Frederick D. Reese of Selma knew first hand about barriers to black voting. He was president of the Dallas County Voters League, an agency working to register black voters. Selma is located in Dallas County.

An educator, Dr. Reese wanted to involve his fellow black teachers in the struggle for voting rights. The soft-spoken but steady crusader was well qualified to lead. Raised in a poor family, the hard work of his young widowed teacher-mother enabled him to go to a black college. He also became a teacher, and in 1989 achieved the distinction of being named principal of an integrated Selma high school. But in 1965, he—like his black brothers and sisters—was no stranger to the backs of buses, separate water fountains, and a rigid system that kept even many of his well-educated teacher colleagues off the voting rolls.

Reese saw the momentum that teachers could give to the voting rights struggle. Teachers represented the single largest group of professional black people. Dr. Reese sent out the call for black teachers to meet at one of the black schools. From there, he told them, they would march to the courthouse and demand the right to be registered. For in Selma at the time, with its population of about 28,000 people—more than half of them black—only 335 blacks were registered voters.

On the afternoon of January 22, Dr. Reese led the teachers from the school, past the black housing settlements, and to the Dallas County Courthouse. Along the way, black parents, with tears flowing down their cheeks, watched as their children's teachers marched past. And young students cheered and waved, recognizing the people they usually saw only at the front of their classrooms.

At the courthouse, the teachers were turned back after an unpleasant confrontation with county authorities. But the teachers' march gave momentum to the voter registration campaign. It helped lead to a bigger march.

7

Setting Out for Montgomery

Many local marches for voting rights were producing no results for black people—except confrontations, often bloody, with the police. Black leaders realized that one large demonstration was needed to focus attention on voter registration problems. They planned a big 50-mile march from Selma to Montgomery, Alabama's capital.

Dr. Reese was responsible for arrangements for the Montgomery march. The line formed in front of Selma's Brown Chapel A.M.E. Church. The city had an ordinance that required marchers to walk at least three feet apart. Dr. Reese reminded the marchers to observe the rule carefully. Not to do so would mean arrest.

Sunday, March 7, 1965. It was a gray but warm and breezy day. At one o'clock that afternoon, about 600 marchers set out from the church. Some were singing the National Anthem and "We Shall Overcome," the most popular protest song of that era. Others talked excitedly. Neighbors cheered as the marchers made their way down the street. But the cheering stopped when Wilson Baker, Selma's Public Safety Director, ordered the marchers to return to the church.

Brown Chapel A.M.E. in Selma

Senator Edmund Pettus

The marchers did not return. They continued, finally reaching the Edmund Pettus Bridge, which crosses the Alabama River at the edge of Selma. The bridge has a high flat crest in the middle so that people cannot see the other side until they get to the end of the bridge.

As Dr. Reese and the marchers reached the end of the bridge, they looked down on a "sea of blue"—blue helmets, blue uniforms, and the blue and gray cars of state troopers parked on each side of the highway. The troopers wore gas masks and had nightsticks poised in front of them, ready to hold back the marchers. The city limits of Selma ended at the bottom of the bridge. Once the marchers would get beyond that point, they would be on

State Highway 80, where the state troopers had jurisdiction.

Sheriff Jim Clark and his posse, as the county authorities, also were ready to hold back the marchers. "This is an unlawful assembly," the sheriff announced through a bullhorn. "You are to disperse and return to the church."

The marchers continued. They did not talk. They had made a commitment to march, unless they faced force. This commitment was so intense that it overcame fear. In their hearts they were ready for anything. Many began praying as they approached the police line.

"You have two minutes to disperse," came the voice again. No one moved.

Then came the order: "Troopers advance."

The troopers moved on the crowd. Holding their night-sticks at both ends, they pushed against the marchers. Then, the police began swinging the clubs at the people. Blood was soon spurting from head wounds. Women were not spared. The air was filled with screams of horror and terror. The sheriff's posse on horseback now closed in, their whips cracking across the backs of the protestors. Troopers rolled and lobbed tear gas into the crowd.

Edmund Pettus Bridge

In panic, some of the marchers ran back across the bridge; others huddled behind a building in a nearby open field. The troopers regrouped, then formed a line from the center of the building to the bridge. They had the marchers trapped. Near the end of the line was the sheriff's posse on horseback. The state troopers held the line but the sheriff's posse struck people's heads and shoulders as they tried to flee across the field. The posse then hotly pursued the stricken blacks, running them down.

When ambulances were finally permitted to attend to the injured, more than 50 people were taken to the local hospital.

Special reports of the bloody affair were flashed across the nation's TV screens. Early newscasts called the attack "An Assault on Highway 80." Later, it was called "Bloody Sunday." Most Americans didn't like what they saw on TV. They knew a change had to come.

8

All the Way to Montgomery

When Dr. King heard the news, he called Dr. Reese from Atlanta. Getting a first hand report, Dr. King promised to send help immediately. Within a few hours, he had hundreds of telegrams flashing across the country, calling for "...clergy of all faiths...to join me in Selma for a ministers' march to Montgomery on Tuesday, March 9th."

To ensure the marchers' safety, Dr. King expected to have a restraining order by Tuesday against the officials who had stopped the earlier march.

About nine o'clock that evening, a mass meeting was held at the Brown Chapel Church. Some white ministers from New Jersey had already arrived. "We're here to help," they told the congregation, "to give our assistance, to march, to give of ourselves for your cause."

More clergy came from other states. Almost all denominations were represented, adding new strength to the cause. The black marchers had hope again. White people as well as black would now push for equality. As preparations were made for the march, Dr. King and the other ministers stressed the importance of maintaining nonviolence no matter how great the provocation.

On Tuesday, the march started again, with Dr. King in the lead. The crowd approached the Edmund Pettus Bridge singing, "Ain't Gonna Let Nobody Turn Me Round." But as the marchers reached the crest of the bridge, their eyes once again fell on the sea of blue uniforms and helmets. All fell silent.

Major John Cloud, in charge of the state troopers, used his bullhorn to order the marchers to stop.

"We have a right to march to Montgomery," Dr. King replied.

When Cloud repeated his order, Dr. King asked if the marchers could pray. The major agreed but said that the marchers would then have to return to their church.

Several of the clergy said prayers. When the kneeling marchers stood up, Dr. King told the people to turn around and return to the Brown Chapel. Peacefully, the marchers retraced their steps. In the meetings that followed in the church, Dr. King reassured the marchers that he would lead them to Montgomery.

That evening, the Reverend James Reeb, one of the first white ministers to arrive, had dinner with some friends. After dinner, his group made a wrong turn in the road and was attacked by four white men. The minister

Civil Rights march from Selma to Montgomery

suffered a massive skull fracture that required immediate attention, but hours went by before he reached the hospital. By then it was too late to save his life.

Dr. Reeb's murder made front page news. Almost everywhere in the country, people held church services for him. And plans went forward quickly for the promised march to Montgomery.

Governor Wallace, determined to stop the march, flew to Washington to confer with President Johnson. The governor finally agreed to let the march proceed. Then the president spoke to the American people. "It's really all of us," he said, "who must overcome the crippling legacy of bigotry and injustice. And," he concluded, "we shall overcome."

To protect the marchers, the president signed an order. It federalized nearly 1,900 men of the Alabama National Guard, and authorized 2,000 more regular army troops.

Sunday, exactly two weeks after "Bloody Sunday," dawned bright and clear, with the federal troops in their places. The stage was set. Shortly after noon, about 8,000 marchers left Brown Chapel. By the end of the day, many of the initial supporters had to return home. A smaller group would continue the march.

Many white people along the route protested with crude signs and racist taunts, but this time, no forbidding troopers stood in the way. The road was clear all the way to Montgomery.

Dr. Reese had done much planning behind the scenes to ensure that the march would move smoothly and that marchers' needs would be met. A shuttle bus was provided so that people could march one day and return to their jobs the next. A big tent was set up for the marchers who needed a place to sleep, and rest stops were arranged in private homes along the way. Big trucks brought in food.

As the march approached Montgomery, its ranks began to swell. Thousands wanted to be part of making civil rights history. When the marchers reached Montgomery's city limits, a huge rally was held with celebrities providing entertainment. Sammy Davis, Jr., a black entertainer, and Peter, Paul, and Mary, folksingers popular at the time, were among the celebrities.

The fifth and final day of the march was a joyous one. Reaching the center of Montgomery, nearly 25,000 people walked down Dexter Avenue. They passed Dr. King's old church, where the bus boycott had been planned ten years before. Now the marchers watched Dr. King climb the broad steps of the Capitol Building, and they listened as he spoke. There would be many more bridges to cross on the road to freedom, he told them, but he also challenged them to patience and nonviolence on the journey.

The crowd slowly began to go its way. Airplanes, buses, and cars carried marchers in all directions. But all was not yet over. A white woman who had been transporting marchers was shot that final night. Mrs. Viola Liuzzo,

President Lyndon B. Johnson hands Dr. Martin Luther King the pen used in signing the Voting Rights Act on August 6, 1965.

a housewife from Detroit, had gone to Alabama to help the demonstrators. While driving home that night, she was shot and killed by Klansmen driving past her car.

The need for racial justice was clear to most of the nation. Six months later, Congress passed the Voting Rights Act of 1965. When President Johnson signed the bill into law, he said, "Today is a triumph for freedom as great as any victory that's ever been won on any battlefield."

The years that have followed the passage of America's great civil rights laws have not always been easy. There have been both victories and continued challenges to the full realization of equality for black Americans. Racism

A black teacher with some of her students near the Edmund Pettus Bridge in Selma

still exists in America, and not just in the South. Economic opportunity is not always accessible to all citizens. But we can appreciate that much progress has been made in America's goal of justice for all citizens. Black people have benefited from new educational, social, and employment opportunities. The right to vote has allowed many more black people to participate in U.S. political life on the national, state, and local levels. America has come a long way since Montgomery's black people endured a year's inconvenience during their boycott to secure fair treatment on local buses. But the quest for racial justice and harmony continues. Every generation must do its part to build on gains already made.

9

A Visit to Montgomery

Montgomery is a city full of history, beginning with its name. It was named after a Revolutionary War hero, General Richard Montgomery. Not only is the name historic, it is also easier to pronounce than "Chunnanugga Chatty"! That's the name it was given by the Native Americans who roamed the Montgomery area before the arrival of white people.

Montgomery was the capital of the Old South—it became the first capital of the Confederacy. It also has been a bridge to modern American life—it saw the beginning of the national movement for black civil rights. With its wide range of the old and the new, there is much to see in Montgomery.

Dexter Avenue, in the center of the city, gives a quick but rich glimpse of Montgomery's history. At one end of the avenue is an artesian well. Now known as Court Square Fountain, it has been used since Montgomery was founded in 1819. Residents used to dip big buckets into the well to get water for their horses and for use in their nearby homes. The well was also the business center of town. Cotton and other products, as well as slaves, were auctioned by the well. In 1885, the open fountain was topped off with ornate statuary.

During the Selma to Montgomery march, demonstrators passed the fountain on their way to the Capitol Building. Ten years earlier, Mrs. Rosa Parks boarded a bus across the street from the fountain. Her refusal to give up her seat to a white person led to the city bus boycott.

Walk along Dexter Avenue toward the Capitol Building, which is located at the other end of the avenue. On the right, you'll pass the Dexter Avenue King Memorial Baptist Church, where Dr. King served his first pastorate. During that time, he began his leadership as the driving force behind the civil rights movement. It was in the basement of this church that the meeting was held in 1955 during which the decision was made to launch the boycott. A large mural in the church, pictured on the cover, depicts major events in the civil rights movement and Dr. King's life.

Before you get to the Capitol, turn right and walk a block to the Civil Rights Memorial. The monument honors 40 men, women, and children who gave their lives from 1954 to 1968 in the struggle for racial equality. Their names, date, and place of death are engraved on a 12-foot

Civil Rights Memorial in Montgomery

circular black granite table. People can touch the names through a light stream of water that flows evenly over the top of the table. Inscribed on an adjacent wall, which also has a thin sheet of water running over it, are the words from the Bible that Dr. King often quoted. Dr. King said that black people would not be satisfied "...until justice rolls down like waters and righteousness like a mighty stream."

The plaza surrounding the Memorial is a thoughtful place. The sound of the monument's water is peaceful, its coolness refreshing on hot Alabama days. The monument stirs our reflection about the struggle for equality, about how far our country has come in its quest, and how far it yet has to go.

The monument was designed by Maya Lin, who also created the Vietnam Veterans Memorial in Washington, D.C.

Capitol building in Montgomery

At the end of Dexter Avenue is the sparkling white Capitol Building of the state of Alabama. It is one of only a few U.S. state capitols to be designated a National Historic Landmark. A bronze star marks the spot where Jefferson Davis stood in 1861 to take the oath of office as President of the Confederate States. Dr. King stood on the same steps when he addressed 25,000 people at the end of the historic Selma to Montgomery march.

A block from the Capitol is the Alabama Archives and History Museum. It's a fine museum, with its collections of artifacts from Alabama history. The state's early Native American inhabitants, military history, and 19th-century life from quilts to medicine are but a few of the exhibits. It's also fun to venture into "Grandma's Attic," a special children's gallery that features everything from toys to antique sewing machines. In this "hands-on" gallery, you're free to touch the items—the way you might in a real grandma's attic!

Two other interesting museums, from a number of them in the city, are the Montgomery Museum of Fine Arts, with its excellent collection of paintings by southern artists; and the Lurleen Wallace Museum, honoring Alabama's first woman governor.

Not far from the Capitol Building is the Old Alabama Town Historic District. It's one of several historic districts in Montgomery. Alabama Town, a restoration of more than three blocks of buildings and landscapes, shows how people lived in Alabama in the 1800s. Visit a pioneer homestead, a pole barn and log cabin, and an elegant townhouse. A one-room schoolhouse shows where yesterday's children learned their ABCs. Tour guides at the schoolhouse like to tell you, "History is alive at Old Alabama Town." Then, with a chuckle they inform you, " 'History' is the name of a cat that roams around the grounds!"

In nearby Union Station, one of the first Lightning Route Trolleys is on display. It was part of the nation's first system of trolleys—electric street cars—that rumbled along tracks on Montgomery streets in the late 1800s. It was called the Lightning Route because of its tremendous—for then—speed. It went six miles an hour! The Lightning Trolley replaced the old mule-drawn trolleys.

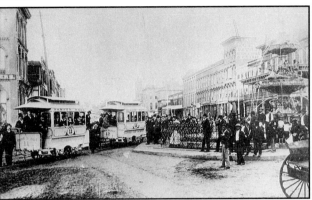

Loading cotton bales on Alabama River boat

Trolley cars near Court Square Fountain near the turn of the century

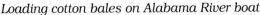

Today you can ride along the Old Lightning route in a bus that somewhat recreates the original trolley.

While you're in the neighborhood of Union Station, walk around outside, where you'll see the Alabama River make a wide curve. The river, its dock, and the rich surrounding farmland made Montgomery the trade and transportation center of the region. Cotton was a major crop in the South for many years. Millions of tons of it were grown on Alabama's vast plantations and picked by slaves, then baled and shipped from Montgomery to coastal Mobile, Alabama, to be sent to foreign ports. Many old warehouses where the cotton was weighed and stored are still near Union Station. Though some cotton is still grown in Alabama, Montgomery today is the largest cattle market in the Southeast.

The Executive Mansion is the residence of Alabama governors. It is a fine example of the grandeur found in southern plantation homes, even though this mansion was built after the Civil War. Sometimes visitors get a bonus if they're lucky—occasionally the governor takes time to meet sightseers and guests.

Another home important in the history of Montgomery—and the entire South—is the White House of the Confederacy. President Davis and his family moved into this fine southern house in 1861. They enjoyed giving many elegant dinners and receptions in the beautiful building. Women guides wearing long dresses tell you interesting stories about President and Mrs. Davis.

A place near Montgomery that visitors enjoy is Maxwell Air Force Base. On this site in 1910, Orville and Wilbur Wright operated the world's first flight training school. The stainless steel Monument to Powered Flight is a reminder of the Wright brothers' trailblazing efforts in aviation history. Maxwell is also the home of the Air University, a major Air Force education center. It includes the largest military library in the Department of Defense. The base also has exhibits of military aircraft.

Save an afternoon for the Montgomery Zoo. With more than 600 animals, it features a giant walk-through bird cage, Australian exhibits, a growing chimpanzee family,

Confederate White House, home of Jefferson Davis

and America's only exhibit of bears and coyotes living together in harmony.

Montgomery, a busy city of about 200,000 people, also has many beautiful gardens and parks, theaters and halls that present a wide range of programs, sports events, and riverboat cruises on the Alabama River, to name a few of the many other activities available to visitors.

Once you're there in central Alabama, try to make time to visit Selma, 50 miles west of Montgomery. From Montgomery, take Highway 80, a graceful drive with moss-draped trees along the way. This is the route of the historic march from Selma to Montgomery. Use your imagination to hear the marchers singing and talking,

Rural scene from central Alabama

and the federal troops guarding the marchers' way. You'll soon arrive in the little town of Selma, high above the rolling waters of the Alabama River.

The big bridge at the edge of town is the Edmund Pettus Bridge. It looks the same today as it did in 1965 when the marchers walked across and beheld the "sea of blue," the state troopers at the other end of the bridge. The bridge was named for General Pettus, a general in the Confederate Army, and later a U.S. Senator.

The Selma Chamber of Commerce has a cassette that guides visitors through Selma's historic district. You'll see Dallas County Courthouse, where decisions were made to stop the civil rights marchers, and where many attempts were made by blacks to register to vote. You'll also see the

Brown Chapel A.M.E. Church where Dr. King set out on the famous march to Montgomery. The Dr. Martin Luther King Monument is located in front of the church.

Selma was also the site of a Civil War battle. You can see some remnants of the 100-building complex of the Selma Gun Foundry. In a fiery siege, Union troops destroyed the arsenal, factories, and much of the city. Visit the Old Depot Museum and the Joe T. Smitherman Building Museum to see locally-made munitions and other war relics, as well as artifacts of Native Americans who lived in the area.

Each spring, there is a Civil War battle re-enactment during Selma's Cahawba Festival, an event that recalls the time when the old city was, for a brief time, the capital of Alabama. You can tour Selma's historic homes and buy original handcrafts along the riverfront market. Here you'll also find places to eat catfish, a southern specialty.

When you visit Montgomery and Selma, you are in the heart of the Deep South. Montgomery has been called Center Stage in the South. From capital of the Confederacy to cradle of modern civil rights, the city has been in the forefront of southern life. It is a memorable place to visit.

Index